Giant Panda

Connect the dots from **A** to **E**. Color.

Polly Panda came from China.

Giraffe

Connect the dots from **a** to **e**. Color.

Georgia Giraffe is eating leaves for lunch!

FS-11072 Zoo Dot-to-Dot

Anteater

Connect the dots from **A** to **H**. Color.

Annie Anteater is eating ants.

© Frank Schaffer Publications

FS-11072 Zoo Dot-to-Dot

Pelican

Connect the dots from **a** to **h**. Color.

Peter Pelican would sure like a nice fish to eat!

Bactrian Camel

Connect the dots from **A** to **M**. Color.

A camel's hump is really a lump of fat!

Dromedary Camel

Connect the dots from **a** to **m**. Color.

Would you like to take a ride on me?

FS-11072 Zoo Dot-to-Dot

Zebra

Connect the dots from **A** to **P**. Color.

Can you color all of my stripes.

FS-11072 Zoo Dot-to-Dot

Kangaroo Rat

Connect the dots from **a** to **p**. Color.

I jump just like a kangaroo!

FS-11072 Zoo Dot-to-Dot

Aardvark

Connect the dots from **A** to **T**. Color.

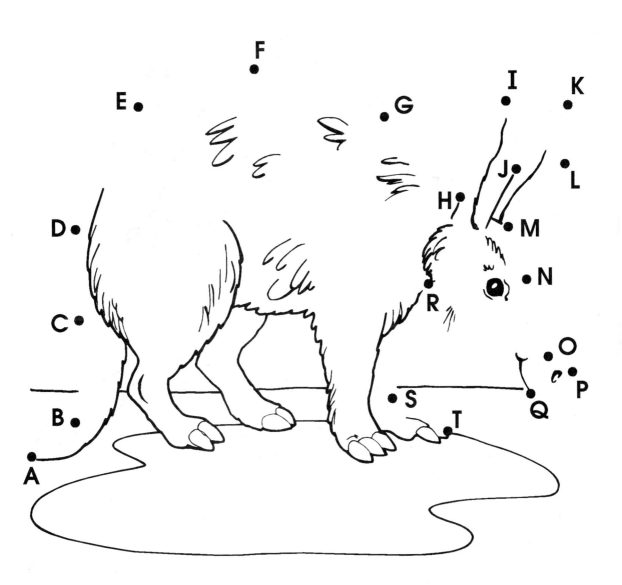

Artie Aardvark always eats ants.

FS-11072 Zoo Dot-to-Dot

Flamingo

Connect the dots from **a** to **t**. Color.

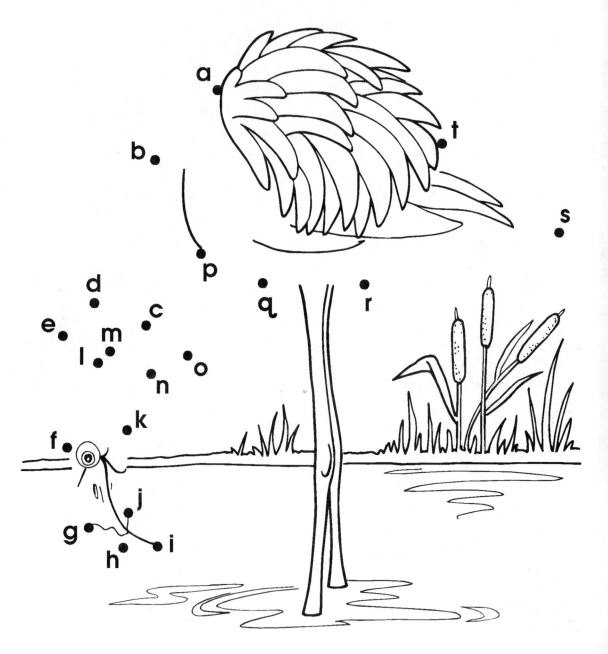

Flora Flamingo lives near lakes, marshes, and seas.

10

FS-11072 Zoo Dot-to-Dot

Chimpanzee

Connect the dots from **A** to **Z**. Color.

Charlie Chimpanzee loves to play!

Bighorn Sheep

Connect the dots from **A** to **Z**. Color.

I am hunted for my horns.

FS-11072 Zoo Dot-to-Dot

Spider Monkey

Connect the dots from **A** to **Z**. Color.

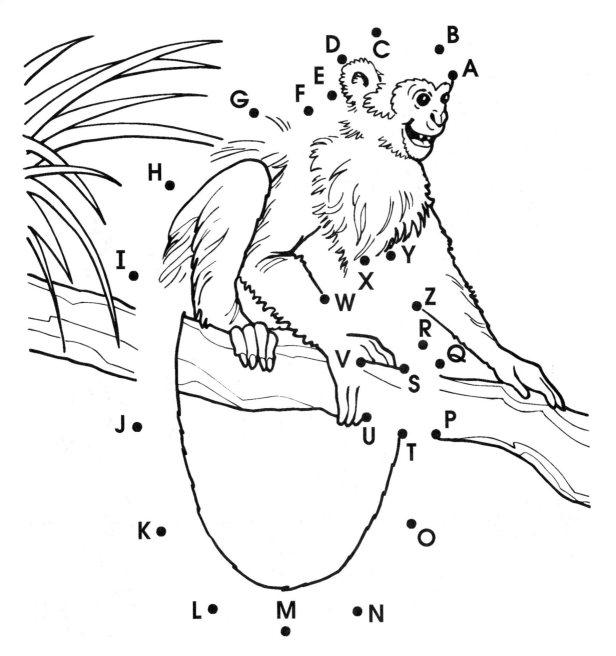

I can hang by my tail!

13

Nile Crocodile

Connect the dots from **A** to **Z**. Color.

I might grow to be over 20 feet long.

FS-11072 Zoo Dot-to-Dot

Salamanders

Connect the dots from **A** to **Z**. Color.

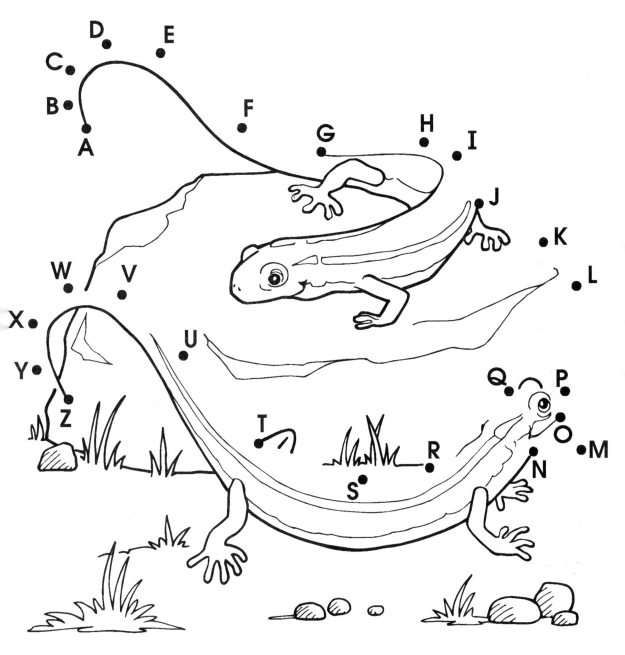

Sam and Sally Salamander eat grubs and slugs.

FS-11072 Zoo Dot-to-Dot

Cheetah

Connect the dots from **A** to **Z**. Color.

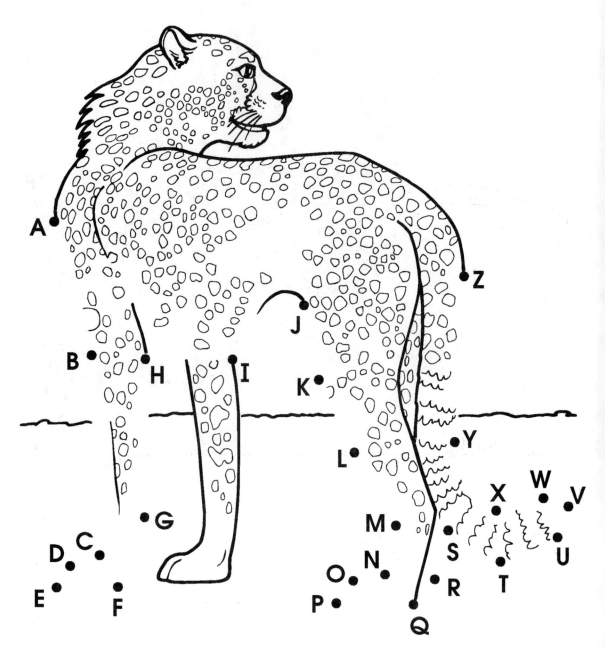

I am the fastest animal!

FS-11072 Zoo Dot-to-Dot

Polar Bear

Connect the dots from **A** to **Z**. Color.

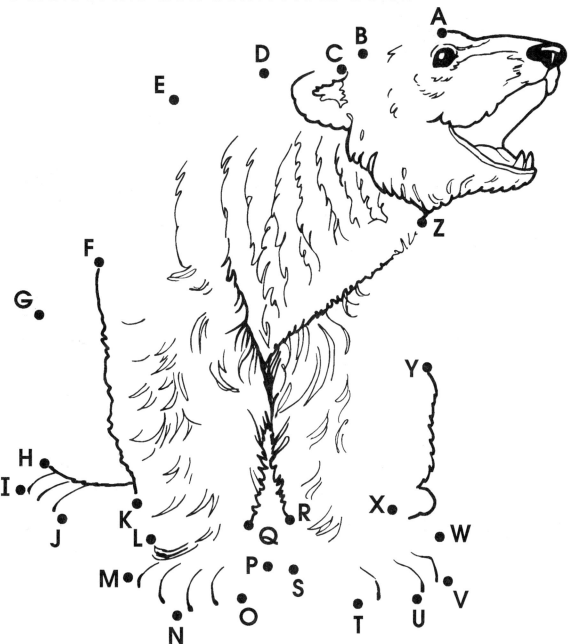

Peter Polar Bear loves to swim and fish.

Orangutan

Connect the dots from **A** to **Z**. Color.

I stay up in the trees almost all of the time.

Lion

Connect the dots from **A** to **Z**. Color.

I like to eat deer, antelope, and zebra.

Rhinoceros

Connect the dots from **a** to **z**. Color.

I love to play in mud or water.

FS-11072 Zoo Dot-to-Dot

Sea Turtle

Connect the dots from **a** to **z**. Color.

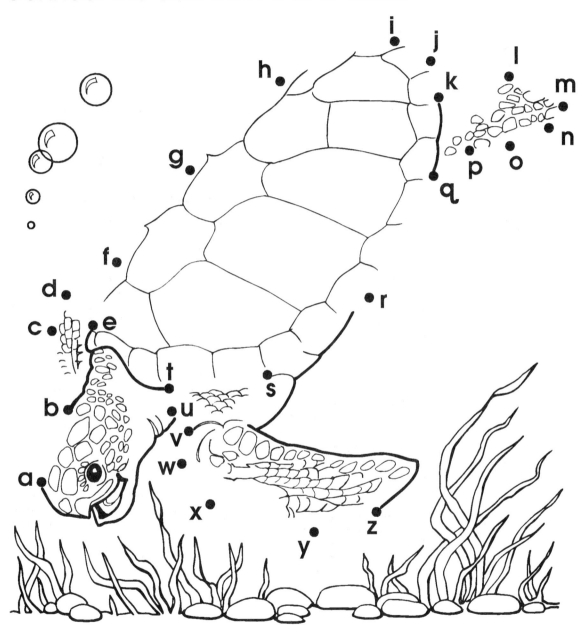

I beat my flippers to swim.

Bald Eagle

Connect the dots from **a** to **z**. Color.

The bald eagle is not really bald.

FS-11072 Zoo Dot-to-Dot

Kookaburra

Connect the dots from **a** to **z**. Color.

My feathers are used to make fishing flies.

Mandrill

Connect the dots from **a** to **z**. Color.

My nose is red and my cheeks are blue.

FS-11072 Zoo Dot-to-Dot

Greater Bush Baby

Connect the dots from **a** to **z**. Color.

This greater bush baby is looking for insects to eat.

Tree Frog

Connect the dots from **a** to **z**. Color.

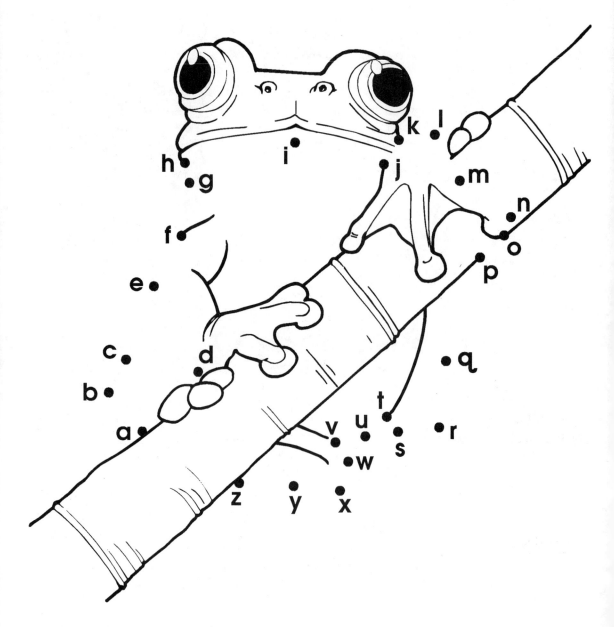

I love to eat earthworms and insects!

FS-11072 Zoo Dot-to-Dot

Moose

Connect the dots from **a** to **z**. Color.

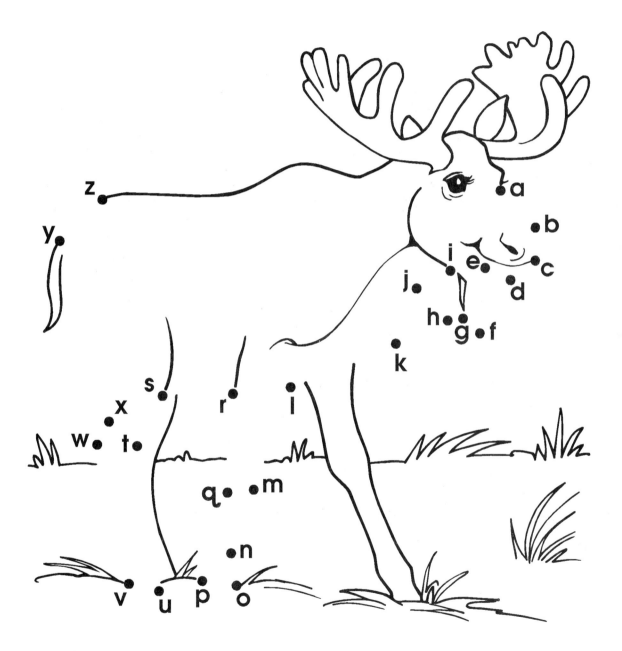

Mickey Moose grows antlers on his head.

27

FS-11072 Zoo Dot-to-Dot

Greater Kudu

Connect the dots from **a** to **z**. Color.

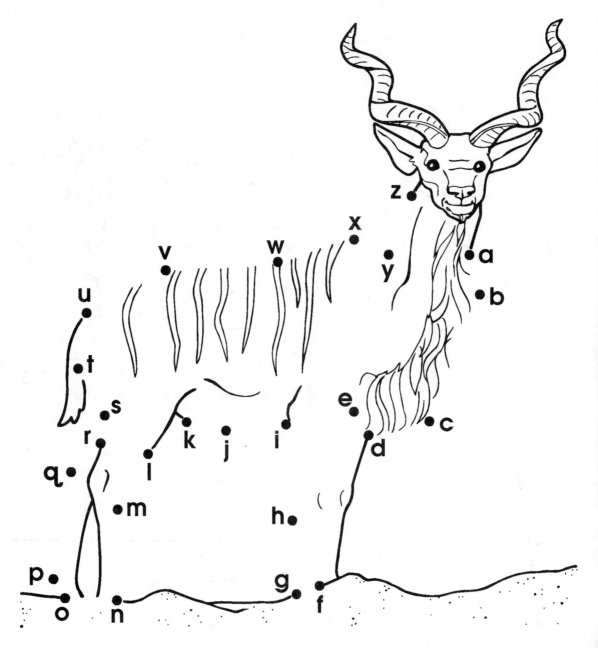

I weigh 600 pounds! I eat grass.

Grizzly Bear

Connect the dots from **1** to **5**. Color.

This great big grizzly bear wants to play!

FS-11072 Zoo Dot-to-Dot

Toucan

Connect the dots from **1** to **5**. Color.

My tongue looks like a feather.

Red Howler Monkey

Connect the dots from **1** to **10**. Color.

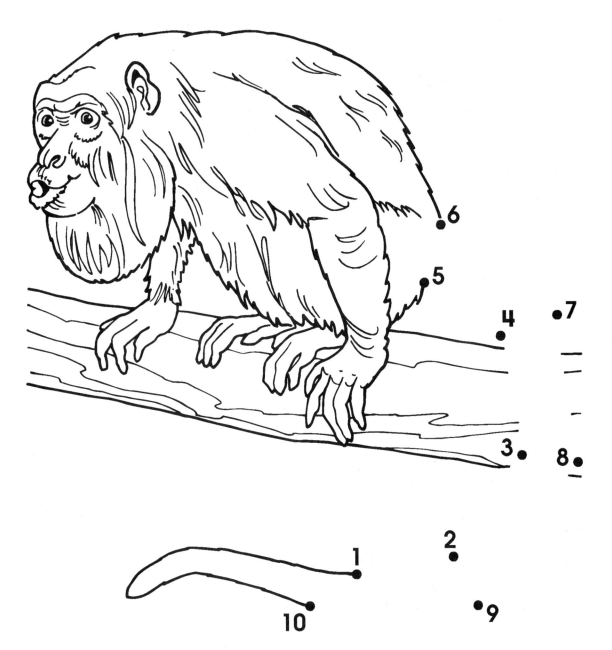

I like to swing by my tail when I eat.

FS-11072 Zoo Dot-to-Dot

Hippopotamus

Connect the dots from **1** to **10**. Color.

I am the third biggest animal that lives on land.

32

Impala

Connect the dots from **1** to **10**. Color.

I love to run and jump.

 FS-11072 Zoo Dot-to-Dot

Sun Bear

Connect the dots from **1** to **10**. Color.

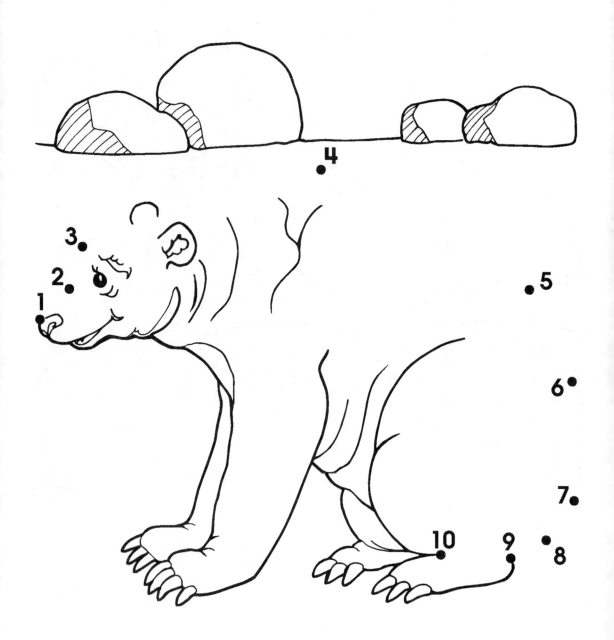

I like to sleep and sunbathe in trees.

FS-11072 Zoo Dot-to-Dot

Walrus

Connect the dots from **1** to **10**. Color.

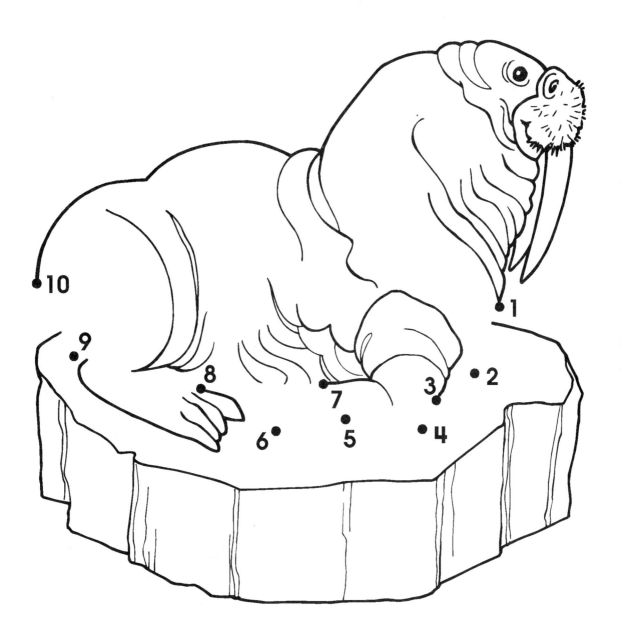

I suck clams from their shells when I am hungry.

Seal

Connect the dots from **1** to **10**. Color.

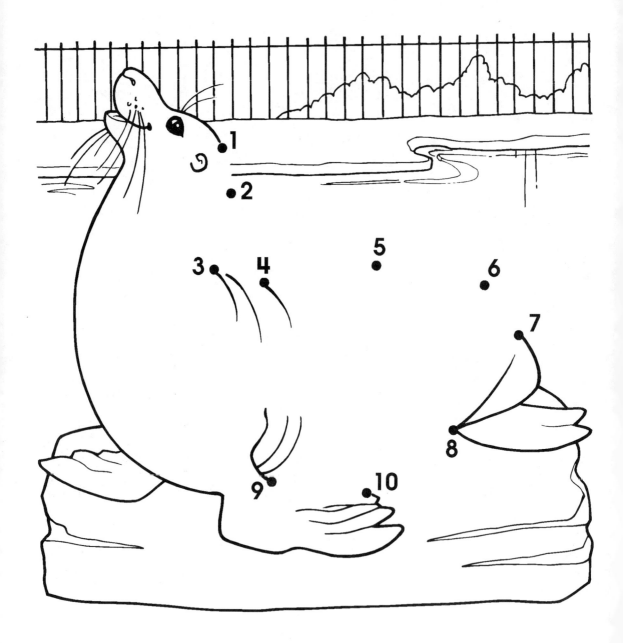

Sammy Seal is looking for fish to eat.

FS-11072 Zoo Dot-to-Dot

Platypus

Connect the dots from **1** to **15**. Color.

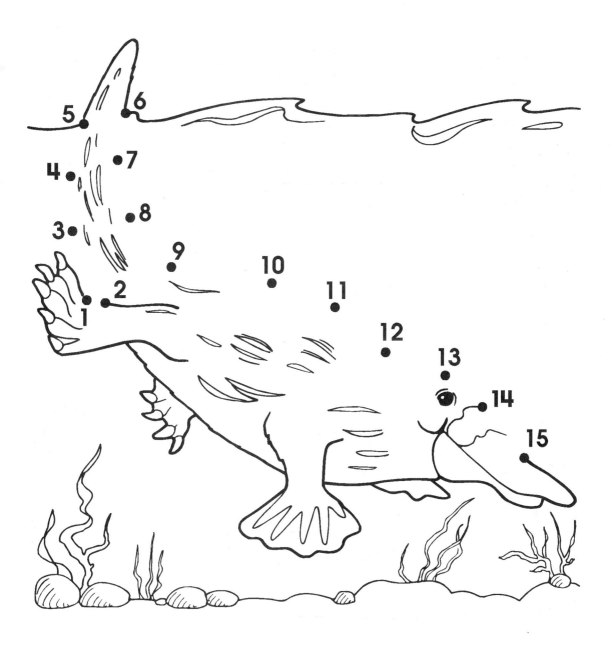

I have feet and a nose like a duck.

Porcupine

Connect the dots from **1** to **15**. Color.

Be careful! My quills can really hurt you!

Okapi

Connect the dots from **11** to **20**. Color.

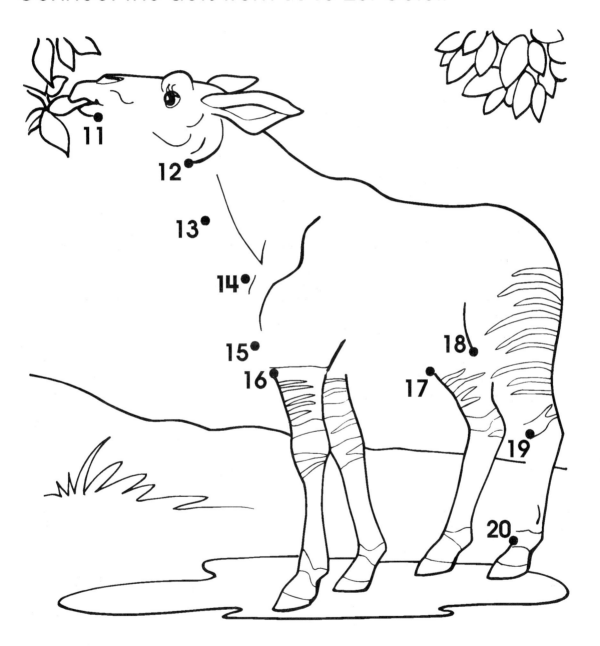

I am red-brown with white stripes and bands.

FS-11072 Zoo Dot-to-Dot

Two-Toed Sloth

Connect the dots from **11** to **20**. Color.

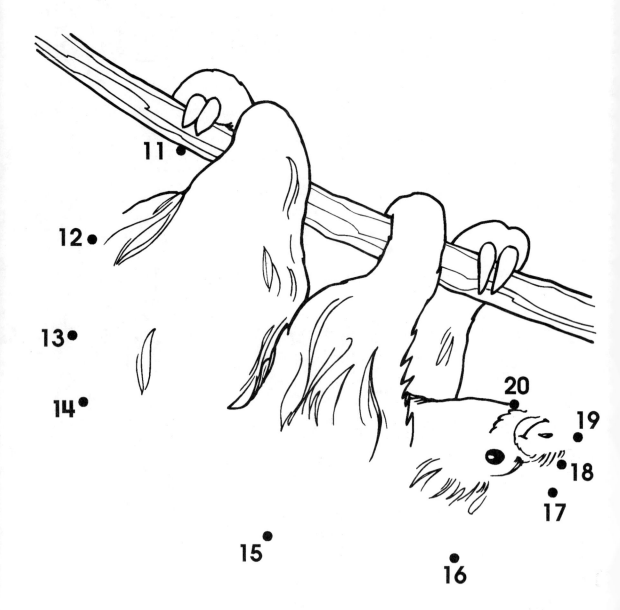

I walk upside down, hanging from branches in trees.

Kiwi

Connect the dots from **11** to **20**. Color.

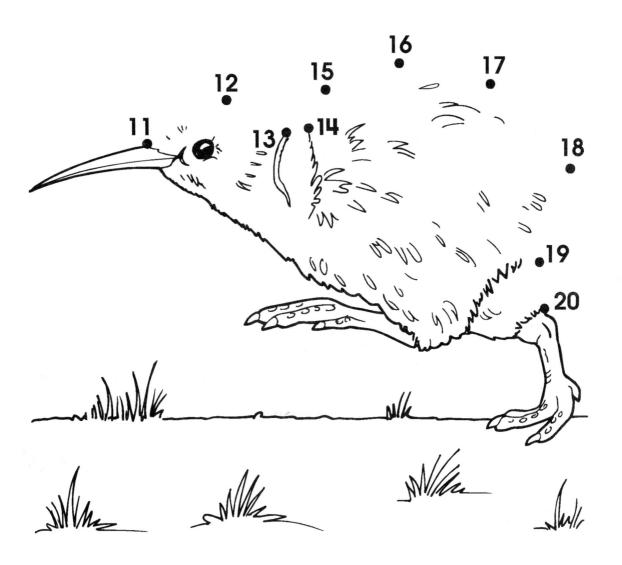

I am a bird, but I cannot fly.

Armadillo

Connect the dots from **11** to **20**. Color.

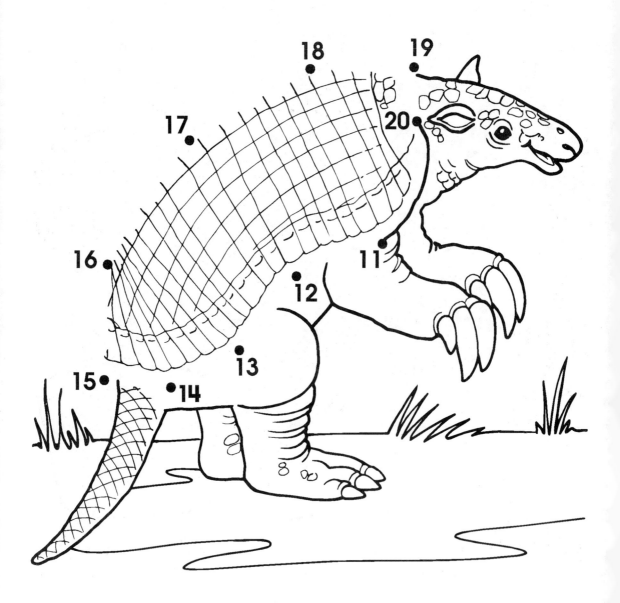

I use my strong claws to dig tunnels in the ground.

FS-11072 Zoo Dot-to-Dot

Musk Ox

Connect the dots from **11** to **20**. Color.

My wool is used to make warm clothing.

FS-11072 Zoo Dot-to-Dot

Otter

Connect the dots from **11** to **20**. Color.

11

12

13

14

15

18

19

16

17

20

I am a great swimmer and diver.

FS-11072 Zoo Dot-to-Dot

Tiger

Connect the dots from **1** to **20**. Color.

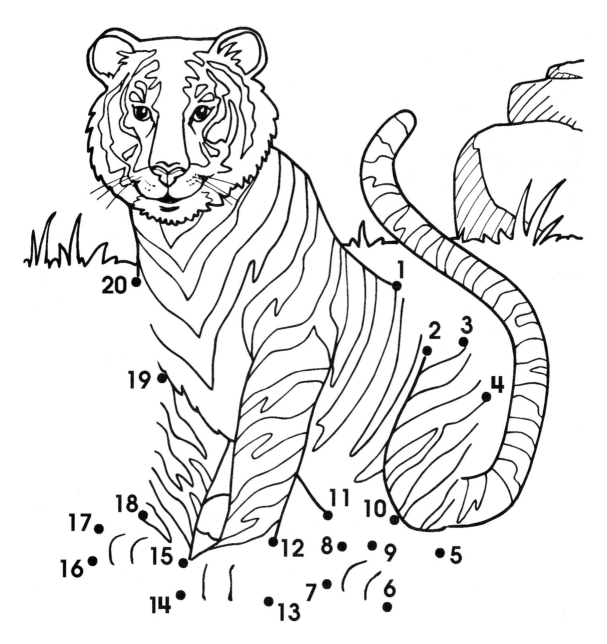

I use my sharp claws to catch my food.

Baboons

Connect the dots from **1** to **20**. Color.

I can carry food in little pockets in my cheeks.

FS-11072 Zoo Dot-to-Dot

Llama

Connect the dots from **1** to **20**. Color.

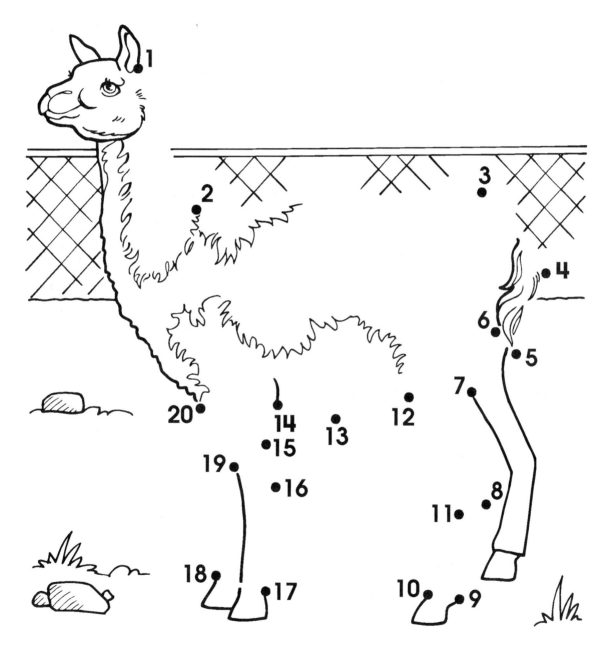

I am strong. I can carry about 100 pounds!

FS-11072 Zoo Dot-to-Dot

Galago

Connect the dots from **1** to **20**. Color.

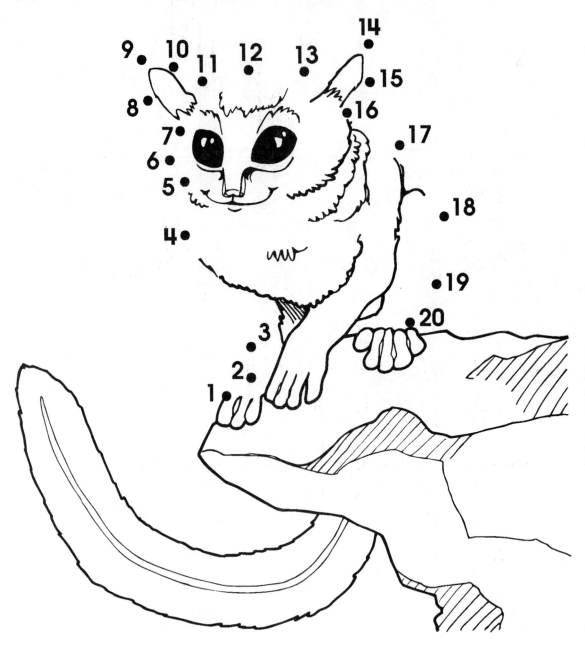

I love to jump very far among tree branches.

FS-11072 Zoo Dot-to-Dot

Ostrich

Connect the dots from **1** to **25**. Color.

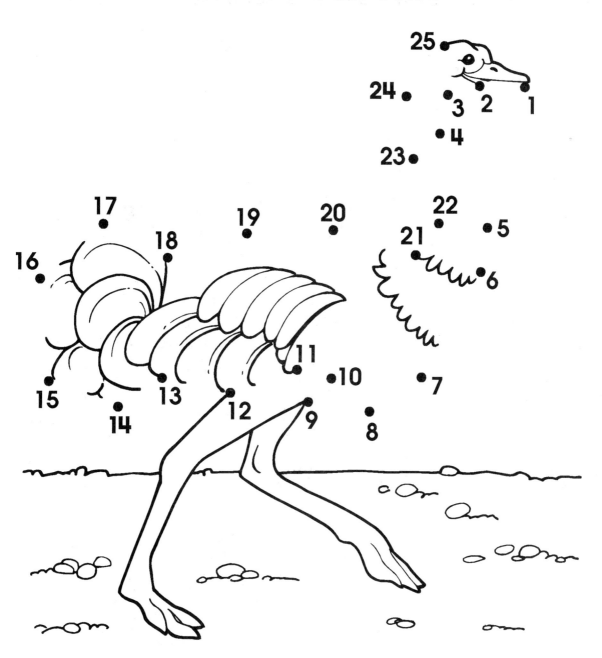

I am the biggest bird of all!

FS-11072 Zoo Dot-to-Dot

Flying Squirrel

Connect the dots from **1** to **25**. Color.

I can glide through the air.

FS-11072 Zoo Dot-to-Dot

Kangaroo and Joey

Connect the dots from **1** to **25**. Color.

A joey is a baby kangaroo. It lives in its mother's pouch for several months.

Emperor Penguin

Connect the dots from **1** to **25**. Color.

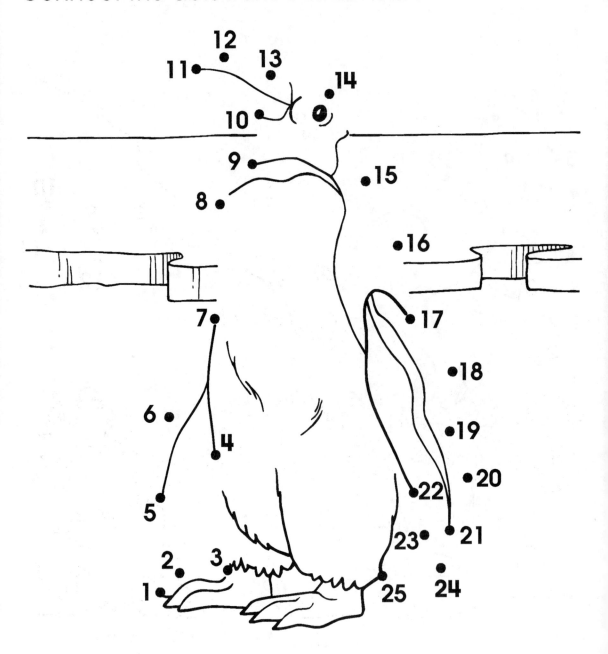

I cannot fly, but I love to swim!

Black Leopard

Connect the dots from **1** to **25**. Color.

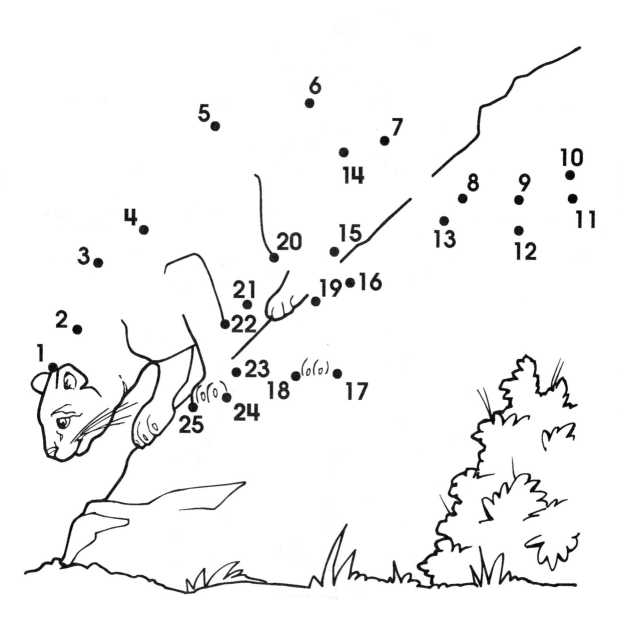

I love to climb trees!

FS-11072 Zoo Dot-to-Dot

Elephant

Connect the dots from **1** to **30**. Color.

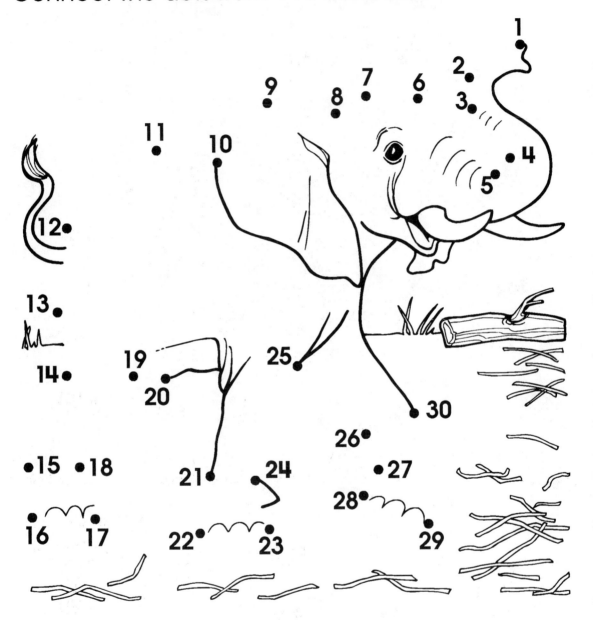

I touch trunks with my elephant friends to say "Hello!"

Gorilla

Connect the dots from **1** to **40**. Color.

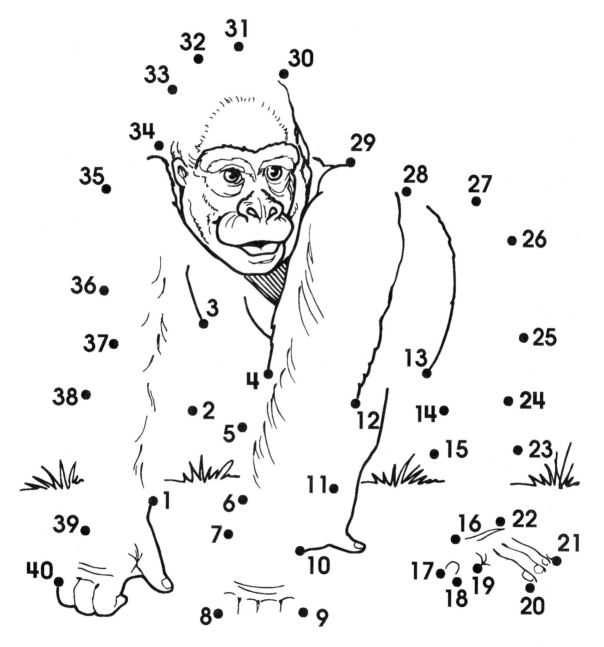

I use my knuckles to help me to walk.

Koalas

Connect the dots from **1** to **50**. Color.

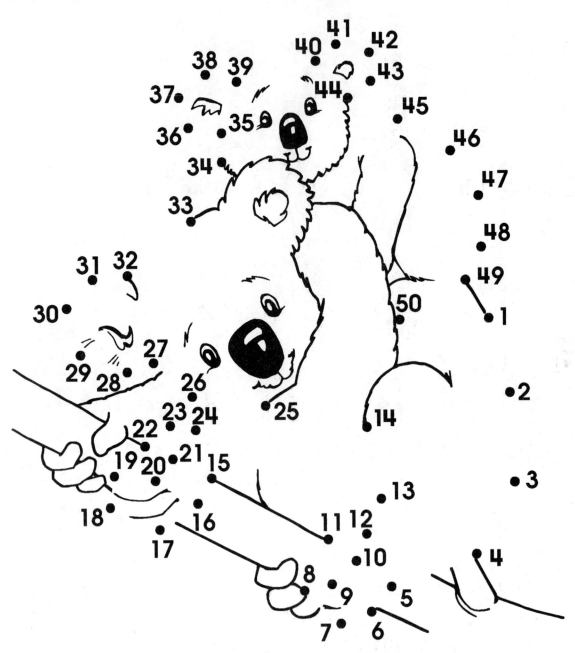

We look like bears, but we are not bears.

FS-11072 Zoo Dot-to-Dot